To:

From:

HOPE IS THE HARVEST

HOPE IS THE HARVEST

Original Insights on Relationships from America's Heartland

PETER REESE

HOPE IS THE HARVEST

The cover features Lucy and Ethel, their work, the author, and his well-traveled laptop.

Photography by Kristen Boom

Copyright © 1997 by Peter Reese

*Published by Garborg's Heart 'n Home, Inc.
P.O. Box 20132, Bloomington, MN 55420*

All rights reserved. No part of this book may be reproduced in any form without permission in writing from the publisher. Printed in USA.

ISBN 1-88130-47-0

HOPE IS THE HARVEST

The author, a small-scale farmer whose priorities are faith, family, and friends, dedicates this Collection to all readers seeking SIMPLICITY, SIGNIFICANCE, and SECURITY.

The reader is encouraged to laugh, contemplate, and compare experiences—and be ready to offer a differing point of view somewhere along the way.

HOPE IS THE HARVEST

*Gratitude.
Appreciation taken
to the next level.*

HOPE IS THE HARVEST

Mercy and compassion are international languages which do not require a translator.

HOPE IS THE HARVEST

A kept promise is more powerful than a brilliant remark or a stunning observation.

HOPE IS THE HARVEST

Honor.
A gift anyone can give
no matter what the occasion.

HOPE IS THE HARVEST

Agreement in all things means at least one of us is not paying full attention to the proceedings.

HOPE IS THE HARVEST

*The three wisest words:
"I don't know."*

HOPE IS THE HARVEST

*Emotions are good followers
but unreliable leaders.*

HOPE IS THE HARVEST

*Compared to being a friend,
any job is easy.*

HOPE IS THE HARVEST

Anger requires little courage and even less planning.

HOPE IS THE HARVEST

*Compassion.
A gift rarely possessed
or displayed.*

HOPE IS THE HARVEST

*Appreciation starts
with observation.*

HOPE IS THE HARVEST

*Communication.
Frequently discussed,
rarely practiced.*

HOPE IS THE HARVEST

Appreciation of our differences starts with the acknowledgment of our similarities.

HOPE IS THE HARVEST

The best immediate reactions are those expressed after thoughtful reflection.

HOPE IS THE HARVEST

*Without strings or bows,
the Stradivarius sounds like
any other violin. It takes teamwork
to make extraordinary music.*

HOPE IS THE HARVEST

Trust.
Years in the making,
moments in the breaking.

HOPE IS THE HARVEST

Intolerance is an acquired distaste.

HOPE IS THE HARVEST

Fewer words reduce the size—and number— of assumptions.

HOPE IS THE HARVEST

*Words bespeak intentions.
Actions express convictions.*

HOPE IS THE HARVEST

To learn, listen.
To understand, watch.
To appreciate, contemplate.
To do none of the above,
speak incessantly.

HOPE IS THE HARVEST

Cooperation sends us squealing "we, we, we" all the way home.

HOPE IS THE HARVEST

*Accountability.
Ask for it by name.*

HOPE IS THE HARVEST

Mercy.
A willingness to withhold when
there is every reason to react.

HOPE IS THE HARVEST

HOME·GROWN WISDOM COLLECTION

To remain a victim is to choose heartache over healing, revenge over reconstruction, and sorrow over sanctuary.

HOPE IS THE HARVEST

Sincerity is not a function of circumstances, surroundings, or situations. Any of these may change in a moment.

HOPE IS THE HARVEST

Kindness transforms hostility to admiration and frustration to appreciation.

HOPE IS THE HARVEST

You can walk a mile in someone else's shoes, but they'll never fit your feet exactly.

HOPE IS THE HARVEST

*Humor.
The WD-40 of relationships,
which stops the creaking and
groaning almost instantly.*

HOPE IS THE HARVEST

Loneliness is often selfishness accompanied by self-righteousness.

HOPE IS THE HARVEST

HOME·GROWN WISDOM COLLECTION

Compromise is valuable in relationships but must be avoided in relationship to values.

HOPE IS THE HARVEST

HOME·GROWN WISDOM COLLECTION

*Words can hurt.
They can also heal,
help, and honor.*

HOPE IS THE HARVEST

HOME·GROWN WISDOM COLLECTION

Compassion is wisdom without words.

HOPE IS THE HARVEST

HOME·GROWN WISDOM COLLECTION

Magnetic personalities are equally strong at attracting and repelling.

HOPE IS THE HARVEST

HOME·GROWN WISDOM COLLECTION

Expectations become dangerous when there are too many of them or they grow to enormous proportions.

HOPE IS THE HARVEST

HOME·GROWN WISDOM COLLECTION

Long-time friends have decided to live with each other's shortcomings.

HOPE IS THE HARVEST

HOME·GROWN WISDOM COLLECTION

*Forgiveness.
It's all practice with no
games scheduled.*

HOPE IS THE HARVEST

HOME·GROWN WISDOM COLLECTION

*Compassion.
Selfishness driven in reverse.*

HOPE IS THE HARVEST

HOME·GROWN WISDOM COLLECTION

Expectations can lead to fulfillment or frustration depending upon their motivation.

HOPE IS THE HARVEST

HOME·GROWN WISDOM COLLECTION

*Spontaneity leads to adventure.
Impulsiveness, to regrets.*

HOPE IS THE HARVEST

HOME·GROWN WISDOM COLLECTION

Fear takes ignorance and uncertainty to new depths. Faith takes hope and courage to unimagined heights.

HOPE IS THE HARVEST

HOME·GROWN WISDOM COLLECTION

Sympathy and empathy both have their place—and their time.

HOPE IS THE HARVEST

HOME·GROWN WISDOM COLLECTION

*Tenderness demonstrates
the strength of forbearance.*

HOPE IS THE HARVEST

HOME·GROWN WISDOM COLLECTION

*Humility.
A quiet conquest of
selflessness over selfishness.*

HOPE IS THE HARVEST

HOME·GROWN WISDOM COLLECTION

Generosity honors people over that which they produce.

HOPE IS THE HARVEST

HOME·GROWN WISDOM COLLECTION

Sacrifice.
Doing more than expected with less
complaining than anticipated.

HOPE IS THE HARVEST

HOME·GROWN WISDOM COLLECTION

Hearing displays courtesy.
Listening demonstrates commitment.

HOPE IS THE HARVEST

HOME·GROWN WISDOM COLLECTION

Jealousy is envy put into immediate action.

HOPE IS THE HARVEST

HOME · GROWN WISDOM COLLECTION

Selfishness is a full-time job without benefits.

HOPE IS THE HARVEST

HOME·GROWN WISDOM COLLECTION

Disagreement.
An opportunity to understand the
other's passions and preferences.

HOPE IS THE HARVEST

HOME·GROWN WISDOM COLLECTION

*Time.
The gift to give someone
who has everything—or very little.*

HOPE IS THE HARVEST

HOME·GROWN WISDOM COLLECTION

The unseen foundation determines how long the visible structure will stand.

HOPE IS THE HARVEST

HOME·GROWN WISDOM COLLECTION

*Grace.
Giving someone more than expected
and not what they deserved.*

HOPE IS THE HARVEST

HOME·GROWN WISDOM COLLECTION

*Forgiveness.
A lost art awaiting
your rediscovery.*

HOPE IS THE HARVEST

HOME·GROWN WISDOM COLLECTION

Do not suffer from truth unspoken, beliefs well hidden, or principles held dear but rarely communicated.

HOPE IS THE HARVEST

HOME·GROWN WISDOM COLLECTION

A diamond is considered brilliant when it reflects the light of its surroundings.

HOPE IS THE HARVEST

HOME·GROWN WISDOM COLLECTION

Dirty doormats are a sign of hospitality.

HOPE IS THE HARVEST

HOME·GROWN WISDOM COLLECTION

We all want to go—and stay—where somebody knows our name.

HOPE IS THE HARVEST

HOME·GROWN WISDOM COLLECTION

Wisdom is bought with tears, joy with kindness, sorrow with selfishness.

HOPE IS THE HARVEST

HOME·GROWN WISDOM COLLECTION

Err on the side of simplicity, be accused of overgenerosity, and gain your reputation among the forgotten.

HOPE IS THE HARVEST

HOME·GROWN WISDOM COLLECTION

Sincerity.
A natural sweetener unequaled
by artificial substitutes.

HOPE IS THE HARVEST

HOME·GROWN WISDOM COLLECTION

A foolish person mistakes the echoes of his own voice for the affirmation of others.

HOPE IS THE HARVEST

HOME·GROWN WISDOM COLLECTION

Bitterness is like a persistent weed. It takes root in the smallest of places under the harshest of conditions.

HOPE IS THE HARVEST

HOME·GROWN WISDOM COLLECTION

A little kindness colors a whole relationship like a single drop of food coloring tints an entire jar of water.

HOPE IS THE HARVEST

HOME·GROWN WISDOM COLLECTION

*Cooperation.
The ideal antidote for isolation.*

HOPE IS THE HARVEST

HOME·GROWN WISDOM COLLECTION

Anger.
A secondary emotion following frustration or disappointment; frequently our primary response.

HOPE IS THE HARVEST

HOME·GROWN WISDOM COLLECTION

When the going gets tough, face-to-face is better than fax-to-fax.

HOPE IS THE HARVEST

HOME·GROWN WISDOM COLLECTION

Hope is trading today's pain for tomorrow's promise.

HOPE IS THE HARVEST

HOME·GROWN WISDOM COLLECTION

Friendship.
Good intentions put into action.

HOPE IS THE HARVEST

HOME·GROWN WISDOM COLLECTION

Pity those who cannot cry, refuse to laugh, or are unable to understand the purpose of either.

HOPE IS THE HARVEST

HOME·GROWN WISDOM COLLECTION

Friendship relies on the ability to demand little from another.

HOPE IS THE HARVEST

HOME·GROWN WISDOM COLLECTION

Empathy.
A willingness to experience unearned
pain without expecting any recognition
or reward for doing so.

HOPE IS THE HARVEST

HOME·GROWN WISDOM COLLECTION

Legacies are gifts only committed people are privileged to share.

HOPE IS THE HARVEST

HOME·GROWN WISDOM COLLECTION

Selfishness.
A game played by one
before a crowd of none.

HOPE IS THE HARVEST

HOME·GROWN WISDOM COLLECTION

Finding faults in others doesn't take a seismograph—we can all do it without special equipment.

HOPE IS THE HARVEST

HOME·GROWN WISDOM COLLECTION

Friends don't let friends live unaccountable lives.

HOPE IS THE HARVEST

HOME·GROWN WISDOM COLLECTION

The self-centered take themselves too seriously. The humble take simple humor from all situations.

HOPE IS THE HARVEST

HOME·GROWN WISDOM COLLECTION

True friends have nothing to prove and even less to lose.

HOPE IS THE HARVEST

HOME·GROWN WISDOM COLLECTION

Forgiveness.
Go first, though none may follow.

HOPE IS THE HARVEST